CW01653946

A Day in Rome

City Explorer

Read With You Center for Excellence
in STEAM Education

Published by Read With You Publishing
Designed by Read With You Center for Language Research and Development
Read With You and associated logos are trademarks and/or registered trademarks of Read With You L.L.C.
ISBN-13: 979-8-88618-133-3
First Edition April 2022
Printed in the United States of America.

Tim is a photojournalist. He takes exciting photos of places around the globe! But he isn't great at remembering names and dates. Today he's in the middle of Italy, visiting a city that is rich in history.

Rosa is a researcher who likes to work from her cozy home office. She is researching Italian history for Tim, and she will want to eat a whole margherita pizza tonight!

IN·HONOREM PRINCIPIS·APOST PAVLVS·V·BVRGHESIVS·ROMANVS·PONT·MAX·AN·MDCXII·PONT

Buongiorno, Rosa! So many places to see, so little time. What can you tell me about this building? The design is gorgeous.

Buon dì! You're at Saint Peter's Basilica. Though you're in the center of Rome, that church is in a separate country called the Vatican City.

T SOLVTVM
ET IN COEL

Another country? Wow. It looks like a lot of people could fit in here. And everywhere I look, I see breathtaking art.

That used to be the largest Christian church in the world. Many people go there to hear the Pope speak and admire the stunning Renaissance art.

I could stare at the pretty walls all day. But I must go on! There's this big museum right by the basilica.

You're in luck! That leads to the Vatican Museums. You'll see more amazing artwork from around the world there.

I've decided I'm moving to
Rome so I can come here every
day! Just look at this ceiling!
This is the Hall of Muses.
Who are they?

You might want to learn Italian
first! The muses were thought to
be magical people who inspired
artists, musicians, and poets.

I feel inspired. And it's only mid-morning! The tourists next to me said they were going to the Castel Sant'Angelo, so I followed them. What is it?

It was meant to be the Roman emperor Hadrian's mausoleum, or fancy tomb. But it became a military fortress and museum.

All this art made me hungry.
What food would you
recommend, Rosa?

Try some *antipasti* and *suppli*!
Antipasti are plates of
meats, cheeses, and olives.
Suppli are rice balls with
mozzarella cheese inside.

Now I'm full of cheese and ready for my next adventure! This big open area is full of hotels and restaurants.

You're in Navona Square. 2,000 years ago, it was a Roman stadium. Now, you can see the Fountain of Neptune in front of you.

M·AGRIPPA·L·F·COS·TERTIVM·FECIT

I keep stopping to take photos, but I think I made it to my next stop. What is the deal with this impressive building?

Pantheon is Greek for *all gods.* It was a temple to honor Roman gods. In the early seventh century, it became a Christian church.

It's gorgeous inside, even 2,000 years after it was built! Does everyone come to admire the beautiful carvings?

Yes, and it also shows off the ancient Romans' engineering skills! That domed ceiling was tricky to build, but it's still standing today.

CLEMENS XII PONT MAX
AQVAM VIRGINEM
COPIA ET SALVBRITATE COMMENDATAM
CVLTV MAGNIFICO ORNAVIT
ANNO DOMINI MDCCXXXV PONTIF VI

I needed a little space after that, and I found another fountain surrounded by tourists!

That's Trevi Fountain, the city's biggest fountain! They say that if you toss a coin in it over your left shoulder, you'll come back to Rome another day.

The more I walk, the more spectacular buildings I see. This one seems modern. I bet the ancient Romans didn't build it.

It's a monument to the first king of all of Italy. Italy had separate states until the mid-1800s, when it became one country.

Wow, I made it to the Colosseum. I've only seen it in pictures, but I know it's famous around the world.

Well, it was a gathering place for fights and executions nearly 2,000 years ago. Imagine it packed with thousands of spectators waiting for violence.

I had no idea what was inside!
I thought it would be a stage,
but I see narrow paths in the
ground and worn-out seats.

The stage used to cover the
paths. People and animals rose
from the trapdoors dramatically!
The circular seating meant
everyone could see.

INSIGNE·RELIGIONIS·ATQVE·ARTIS·MONVMENTVM
VETVSTATE·FATISCENS
PIVS·SEPTIMVS·PONTIFEX·MAX
NOVIS·OPERIBVS·PRISCVM·EXEMPLAR·IMITANTIBVS
FVLCIRI·SERVARIQVE·IVSSIT
ANNO SACRI PRINCIPATVS·EIVS XXIIII

There's so much old stuff around the Colosseum! I see lots of ancient stone roads and buildings, like this arch.

You're at the Roman Forum, an outdoor museum full of ancient things. The Arch of Titus celebrates the ruler who conquered Jerusalem in 71 AD.

The history made me hungry again. Can I end my day with some Italian pasta?

Pasta amatriciana has tomato, cheese, and pork, a yummy combination. Then, grab gelato, a sticky Italian ice cream! You earned it.

Learn

1. What kinds of buildings can you see in Rome?

2. What country is in the middle of Rome?

3. Which is the biggest fountain in Rome?

4. What does *pantheon* mean?

Imagine

1. Which place looks the most interesting to visit? Why?

2. If you could design a fountain, what kinds of statues would you put around it?

3. Which Italian food would you most like to try? Why?

4. Are the buildings in Rome like the old buildings near where you live? How so?

Act

Option 1

Research the Colosseum. Write a paragraph about when and why it was built, and what has happened to it since the Roman Empire. It has been used in many different ways!

Option 2

Build a miniature fountain. Get a big, flat bowl, some clay, and toys that you can get wet. Make your statues with the clay and position the toys in the bowl. Pour a little bit of water inside. You've made your own fountain!

Made in the USA
Monee, IL
29 November 2022

18958678R00024